CW00499743

G.I. Hustlers
Of World War II

By Hugh Hagius

Bibliogay Publications
2011

© *G.I. Hustlers of World War II*, Hugh Hagius 2011

G.I. Hustlers of World War II is available as a paperback printed book or in electronic form as a .pdf file at

Lulu.com/Bibliogay

or at retail outlets.

First Edition: August, 2011
ISBN: 978-0-615-47581-3

All images in *G.I. Hustlers of World War II* are reproduced here in accordance with the Fair Use Law (Per Title 17, United States Code, Section 107); however, these images remain the property of the copyright owners, and will be removed from future printings of this publication upon request. Please address requests to:

hughhagius@gmail.com

or

Bibliogay Publications
P.O. Box 1008
New York, NY 10025

Frontispiece

Contents

Contents

Introduction
By Hugh Hagius

Now that *From Here to Eternity* finally has been published as James Jones originally wrote it, it turns out that Private Angelo Maggio (the Frank Sinatra character) used to let his civilian friend Hal give him blowjobs in return for cash. "Old Hal treats me swell," Private Maggio says. "He's always good for a touch when I'm broke. Five bucks. Ten bucks. Comes in handy the middle of the month."

Frank Sinatra as Private Angelo Maggio

During World War II, a lot of G.I.'s were broke by the middle of the month. A private's pay in 1941 was only $40 a month, and Private Maggio wasn't the only one who found a quick and easy way to make some more.

In fact, it was a time-honored military tradition. Barracks prostitution probably is as ancient as armies. In any case it has a long history.

In the nineteenth-century, Karl Ulrichs, the first gay activist, had a special fondness for the Hussars of Hanover, cavalrymen who sported particularly attractive uniforms. He describes them in high romantic style:

> **...Dear to me down to the heart's depth,**
> **Dearest of all are the young, steel-thewed, magnificent soldiers—**
> **Be it the massive form of a black-browed insolent guardsman,**
> **Or a blue-eyed hussar with the down new-fledged on his firm lip—**
> **Who with clanking spurs and martial tread when they meet me,**
> **Know not how goodly they are, the sight of them how overwhelming.**
> (Translation by John Addington Symonds, quoted in Kennedy, *Ulrichs*, p. 61)

Sailors have their admirers too. So much has been written about them that I don't know where to begin. Think of *Billy Budd*, think of *Querelle*.

Here is an ecstatic tribute to mariners written by Luís Cernuda, the gay poet who fought with the Loyalists in the Spanish Civil War:

> Sailors are the wings of love,
> They are the mirrors of love, the sea's companions,
> And their eyes are bright, like the eyes of love.
> The joyful life coursing through their veins is bright,
> Bright like a glimpse of their bright bare skin.
> Don't let them get away, because a sailor's grin
> Is the beacon of liberty,
> It is a lighthouse beaming over the ocean.
> Yes, a sailor is the ocean, the bright amorous ocean whose sigh is a song.
> Not for me the dull gray city,
> I want only to go to the sea where there waits for me...
> Ship ahoy,
> Anchors aweigh,
> And I float into the bright light.
>
> (*Los Marineros Son Las Alas del Amor*)

A less poetic and more matter-of-fact account of soldierly charms was given by Jennie June, an audacious fairy who was active—very, very active— around New York in the 1890s and early 1900s. She was a frequent guest at several Army forts, and reported:

> I have myself found adolescent professional soldiers the easiest of conquests and the most inclined of any class of men to take the virile part with me. I speak from experience in flirtation with at least two thousand different professional soldiers, only about four hundred of whom, however, went to extremes. I saw not the least tendency toward homosexuality amongst themselves, although I frequented to some extent their barracks and even their bunks. They are only capable of taking the virile part with an individual like your author. In general the common soldiers of the regular army are particularly rough, coarse-grained, vigorous, and sensual men, constituting physically the best blood of the race. Of course many of the nation's fighters have a natural distaste. As just indicated, only about one in five with whom I coquetted went to extremes, while about fifty per cent. of those who knew me by sight would never even speak to me.
>
> Moreover, soldiers lead comparatively idle lives, and also monotonous lives, and these two conditions add to their susceptibility to the wiles of a fairie.
>
> (Jennie June, *Autobiography of an Androgyne*, pp. 117-118)

The Fort Totten Football Team in 1897

Jennie June's favorite haunt was Fort Totten, which has now become Fort Totten Park in Queens. She was very popular at the inter-fort football games. She tells us:

> **In a parade in which my soldier friends took part, I as spectator occupied a rather prominent position on the very edge of the line, and from rank after rank as they passed I distinguished the words: "There's Jennie June." At an inter-fort football game at which there were 500 spectators, amid the continuous shouting, a score got together on my arrival and several times in unison shouted "Jennie June!"**
> *(Autobiography of an Androgyne,* p. 205)

Jennie June also lets us in on the secret of how the fairies practiced their wiles:

> **A man serving at one of those forts told me that common soldiers often speak with one another about their "fairies." Whenever any one of the former appears with a new watch, ring, etc., a common query of his "buddies" is: "Did your fairie give it to you?" Seven out of ten common soldiers appear exceedingly glad to have a prosperous young androgyne in their midst, particularly because he showers them with gifts and entertainment.** (Jennie June, *The Female-Impersonators,* pp. 255-256)

We fast-forward now to England of the 1930s. Our informant is J.R. Ackerley:

His Majesty's Brigade of Guards had a long history in homosexual prostitution. Perpetually short of cash, beer, and leisure occupations, they were easily to be found of an evening in their red tunics standing about in the various pubs they frequented, over the only half-pint they could afford...alert to the possibility that some kind gentleman might appear and stand them a few pints, in return for which and the subsequent traditional tip—a pound was the recognized tariff for the Foot Guards then, the Horse Guards cost rather more—they were perfectly agreeable to, indeed often eager for, a 'bit of fun'...they were young, they were normal, they were working-class, they were drilled to obedience; though not innocent for long, the new recruit might be found before someone else got at him; if grubby they could be bathed, and if civility and consideration, with which they did not always meet in their liaisons, were extended to them, one might gain their affection. (J.R. Ackerley, *My Father and Myself,* pp. 134-135)

Lytton Strachey once concluded a letter to Ackerley by saying "Give my regards to the Army, the Navy and the Police Force."

The Royal Foot Guards

Ackerley's own father had as a young man been a guardsman, and had found a rich patron, who helped him to rise in the business world. Ackerley always wondered whether the patron and his father had been lovers.

So barracks prostitution already was a long established institution when Pearl Harbor was bombed and fifteen million American men were mobilized for duty.

About half of them were drafted right off the farm, most of the others from small towns, and when they got to the big cities they headed straight to the entertainment districts, where the U.S.O. Clubs were situated. These locales also happened to be the red light districts. There they found friendly strangers happy to start up a conversation, offer them a cigarette, and buy them a beer.

During the war years, Tennessee Williams was a regular visitor to Times Square. In his memoirs he recalled making "very abrupt and candid overtures" to groups of sailors or G.I.'s. The overtures were "phrased so bluntly," he said, "that it's a wonder they didn't slaughter me on the spot. They would stare at me for a moment in astonishment, burst into laughter, huddle for a brief conference, and, as often as not, would accept the solicitation, going to my partner's Village pad or to my room at the 'Y.'"

For sea food, Williams frequented Provincetown, and, after the War, Key West.

Guests of Tennessee Williams at Key West

For the more refined, there was the elegant Astor Bar at 45th and Broadway—the very bar memorialized by Cole Porter:

Have you heard about Mimsy Starr?
She got pinched in the Astor Bar.
Well did you evah!
What a swell party this is!

An old-timer told Charles Kaiser, "It was known that if you wanted to get picked up or pick somebody up and it involved money, you went to the Astor Bar, but you went in a suit and a tie. If the hustler wanted some decent money and dinner, he went to the Astor Bar. On the street $10 was a lot, but not in a bar."

By 1948, according to *The Gay Guides for 1949*, the Astor's wartime glory was passé, but the Silver Rail at 43rd and Sixth had large Army and Navy representations.

For those wishing to be even more discreet, there was an unobtrusive brownstone in Brooklyn, a short walk from the Brooklyn Navy Yard, at 329 Pacific Street. Visitors could chat in the parlor with soldiers and sailors and, if the parties came to an agreement, continue the conversation in an upstairs room.

It was all very pleasant until German spies infiltrated the establishment, and attracted the attention of the F.B.I. The police raided in May of 1942; Walter Winchell called it the Swastika Swishery, and the New York Post revealed that a certain Senator X was implicated.

The owner, a man named Gustave Beekman, was promised leniency for cooperating, and he identified Senator David I. Walsh of Massachusetts as one of the regular customers. Senator Walsh, a Democrat, was a bachelor who lived in Boston with his four unmarried sisters.

Senator David I. Walsh

He also was chairman of the Senate Naval Affairs Committee and an isolationist, opposed to the involvement of the U.S. in the war. Franklin D. Roosevelt and J. Edgar Hoover went into action, and very soon Beekman retracted the identification. Senator Walsh ceased to obstruct Roosevelt's plans, and retired at the end of his term.

In spite of all this cooperation Beekman was convicted of sodomy and got the maximum sentence of twenty years. He did not get out of prison until 1963.

All during the war years Alfred C. Kinsey was interviewing men for *Sexual Behavior in the Human Male*, eventually tabulating the responses of twelve thousand individuals and rating them all on a scale from zero to 6—zero meaning no homosexual experience at all, 6 meaning lifelong exclusively homosexual experience.

Kinsey found that only 4 per cent of his subjects scored a rating of 6. (This is close to the per cent of men who today self-identify as gay/bisexual.) About 50 per cent of Kinsey's sample were zeros, engaging in no homosexual activity whatever, and 25 per cent were 1's, meaning only a little fooling around as teenagers.

But that left 21 per cent of his subjects scoring between 2 and 5, meaning that they had significant homosexual experience. That is a ratio of one man out of every five. These men engaged in same-sex contact to the point of orgasm, the conduct occurred after adolescence, and it continued over a period of at least three years or more. The extent of the experience was reflected in the rating number—the 2's not very much, 3's more, 4's even more, and the 5's a lot.

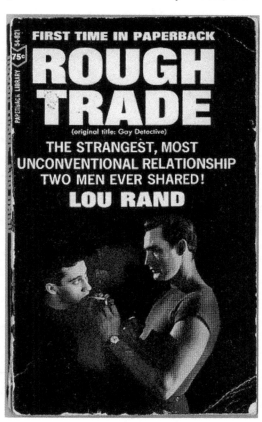

In 1940s gay slang these men were called rough trade. This term did not mean that they were violent or dangerous, just that they were unrefined. Rough trade was working-class men who didn't think of themselves as queer, but would have sex with other men so long as they didn't feel their masculinity was threatened. *The Gay Guides for 1949* says rough trade is "basically a straight one who just likes to be blown."

If you take that proportion of one man in five, the number Kinsey tabulated, as being rough trade, and apply that same ratio to the fifteen million men on active duty during World War II, that gives you three million men like Private Maggio.

Well, yes, some of the men were away fighting the war. Even so there were a lot of 2's, 3's, 4's and 5's out on the town, and plenty of them were susceptible to what Jennie June called the wiles of fairies. They let themselves be blown for a few bucks.

And this didn't stop on V-J Day, because World War II was followed immediately by the Cold War, and the Korean War, and the Berlin Crisis ,and the Cuban Missile Crisis and the Vietnam War, and many other wars and crises, all of them providing a steady supply of broke, horny soldiers and sailors wishing someone would buy them a beer.

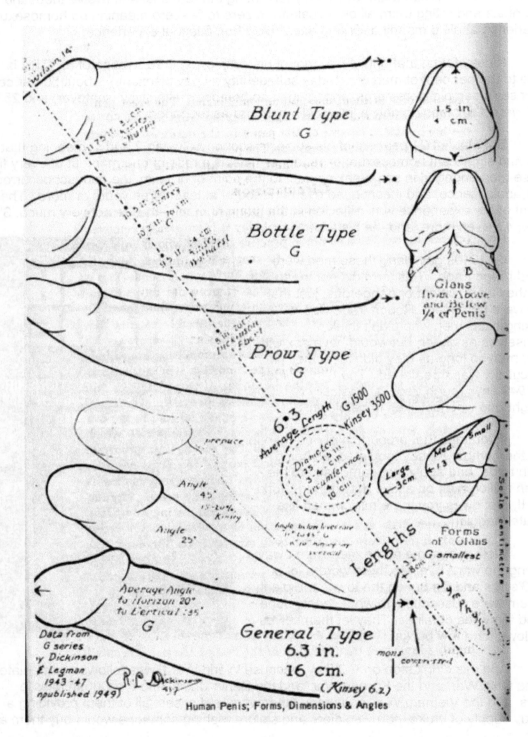

R.L. Dickinson and Gershon Legman drew this graph representing Kinsey's data on penis sizes and shapes.

To be honest, however, there were some mixed feelings on both sides of these transactions. To give you an idea, here are two stories, one from the John's point of view, and another from the hustler's.

"Leo Aultman," interviewed by Charles Kaiser, gives a John's viewpoint:

I was a second lieutenant and I took a four-day pass by myself to get laid. I went to Carmel, California. So lovely. And there was a whole crew of guys there from the cavalry. Which never went overseas because there was no need for a cavalry. But they looked great: jodhpurs and the boots and the whole thing. And there was one who eyed me and I eyed him, and he said he had a room.

When we got there, he said he had to have ten dollars. I said, "Oh?" He said, "Well, I have a date tonight with a girl, so give me ten bucks. Okay?" And I said, "All right"—because he was very attractive. And then he said, "I'm not taking my boots off." And I felt really cheap. He just lowered his trousers. And it was not mutual at all. I just did it and I hated it. And I had to wash afterward, and he said, "Hey, if you want to go again, I'll get undressed for fourteen." And I said, "Not for *two* dollars." And I left. I felt very demeaned. And I never paid again. Ever.

(*The Gay Metropolis*, p. 33)

And here is an account from the other point of view, transcribed from the typescript of *From Here to Eternity* (see facsimile on page 11). Strictly speaking this conversation is fictional, but we can trust James Jones to give us a faithful portrayal of the way soldiers really talked—probably the best portrayal we will get, since they were not much for writing memoirs.

The characters speaking in this passage are Private Angelo Maggio (played in the movie by Frank Sinatra) and Private Robert E. Lee Prewitt (played by Montgomery Clift). They are speaking in a sort of code where preparation means booze and induce means get drunk. It is payday and the two of them are drinking up their pay, but the money is running out, and Maggio is trying to persuade Prewitt to come with him to get some more:

"That's it. Now you got it. Whynt you come out to Waikiki with me later on? This thirteen-fifty will not last forever."

"Maybe I will, after we induce some more. I never did like queers. Every time I get around them I want to punch them in the head."

"Aw, they all right. They just peculiar is all. They maladjusted. Besides, they'll buy you preparation all night long. Just to get to blow you. 'At's a lot of preparation, friend."

"I don't like to be blowed."

Montgomery Clift as Private Prewitt and Frank Sinatra as Private Maggio getting wasted in *From Here to Eternity*; Ernest Borgnine standing.

Angelo shrugged. "Oh all right. I admit it's nothing like a woman. But it's something. Besides, old Hal treats me swell. He's always good for a touch when I'm broke. Five bucks. Ten bucks. Comes in handy the middle of the month."

"Comes in handy payday," Prew said.

Angelo laughed. "This is the first time I been down payday."

"But I still don't like to be blowed."

"Okay. You don't have to. I'll have Hal find one for you and then you just lead her on, for the preparation. Then when you are fully prepared you just get up and stagger home, that's all. Only reason I let Hal blow me is because I got a good thing there. If I turned him down, I'd blow it sky high. And I want to hang on to that income, buddy. Hell, I never smoke nothing but tailormades now. Whynt you come on and go?"

"You think you could find me one?" Prew said, hesitating, yet knowing all the time that he would go.

"Sure. Old Hal'll find one for you. Whynt you come on and go?"

10

"Thats it. Now you got it. Whynt you come out to Waikiki
with me later on? This thirteen-fifty will not last forever."

"Maybe I will, after we induce some more. I never did
like queers. Every time I get around them I want to punch
them in the head."

"Aw, they all right. They just peculiar is all. They
maladjusted. Besides, they'll buy you preparation all night
long." ~~Just to get to blow you. 'Ats a lot a preparation, friend."~~

~~"I dont like to be blowed."~~

~~Angelo shrugged. "Oh, sall right. I admit its nothing
like a woman. But its something. Besides, old Hal treats
me swell. He's always good for a touch when I'm broke. Five
bucks. Ten bucks. Comes in handy the middle of the month."~~

~~"Comes in handy payday," Prew said.~~

~~Angelo laughed. "This the first time I been down payday."~~

~~"But I still dont like to be blowed."~~

~~"Okay. You dont have to. I'll have old Hal find one for~~

~~you and then you just lead her on, for the preparation. Then
when you are fully prepared you just get up and stagger home,
thats all. (Only reason I let Hal blow me is because I got a
good thing there. If I turned him down I'd blow it sky high.
And I want to hang onto that income, buddy.) Hell, I never
smoke nothing but tailormades now. Whynt you come on and go?"~~

"You think you could find me one?" Prew said, hesitating,
yet knowing all the time that he would go.

"Sure. Old Hal'll find one for you. Whynt you come on
and go?"

Prew was looking around the bar. "I already said I'd
go, dint I? Shut up on it. Drop it, for Christ's sake.
Matter of fact, I meant to go all along. I was goin out to
Waikiki to look you up, after I left here. What is this slop
we drinkin anyway?"

James Jones typescript, *From Here to Eternity*
Image Courtesy University of Illinois, Urbana-Champaign,
Rare Book and Manuscript Library.

11

Prew was looking around the bar. "I already said I'd go, dint I? Shut up on it. Drop it, for Christ's sake. Matter of fact, I meant to go all along. I was goin out to Waikiki to look you up, after I left here. What is this slop we drinkin anyway?"
(See facsimile of original typescript, page 11.)

Prew's hesitation, even though he has already decided to go, is a nice touch: "I don't like to be blowed…You think you could find me one?"

But in the previous passage Leo Aultman, the gay man, is just as conflicted: "He was very attractive…I felt very demeaned."

It does great credit to everyone negotiating such difficult terrain that they were able to get it on at all.

US-06-3 JACKSONVILLE' — Handsome ex-serviceman, green eyes, brown hair, 180 lbs., well-hung and game for anything. Would like to write to other handsome males who are equally well-hung. Was just recently discharged from the service. Write a very frank letter, and a photo is a must in first letter!

Of course many others were completely comfortable with the arrangement, and saw the hustler's honorarium as no more sordid than candy and flowers.

Such encounters sometimes could turn into long-term, affectionate relationships, as in the case of Private Maggio's fond, although not very romantically expressed, feelings about Hal: "Old Hal treats me swell… I let Hal blow me because I got a good thing there." (Private Maggio doesn't think he is queer, but really, you know, he is.)

So it was that millions and millions of soldiers and sailors far from home, swept up in the emergency of war and perhaps soon to face bombs and bullets, had sex with other men. Sometimes they did it for fun, sometimes they did it for affection, sometimes they did it for five or ten dollars, and sometimes they did it for all of these reasons.

When they mustered out of the service, back they went to their wives and sweethearts, and their wartime encounters were buried in a very private region of memory. These stories never made it into the grand narrative of national struggle.

This national amnesia was enforced by a system of public morality that actively suppressed these memories, as you can see from the facsimile of Jones's original typescript, reproduced on page 11.

Scribner's demanded a lot of cuts. James Jones was a serious writer who wrote from his own experience and was scrupulous about accuracy, so he resisted. Scribner's brought in a lawyer and for six weeks Jones worked with him, arguing over every word. The lawyer counted in the text 259 occurrences of the word fuck. Then Jones and his editor trimmed the fucks to 146. But the lawyer only allowed them 26.

The gay references of course had to go. In the facsimile you can see two stages of editing. In the first pass, sentences containing the offending words blow and blowed were cut, but on the second pass more than half the passage was crossed out, leaving just this:

"That's it. Now you got it. Whynt you come out to Waikiki with me later on? This thirteen-fifty will not last forever."

"Maybe I will, after we induce some more. I never did like queers. Every time I get around them I want to punch them in the head."

"Aw, they all right. They just peculiar is all. They maladjusted. Besides, they'll buy you preparation all night long."

"You think you could find me one?" Prew said, hesitating, yet knowing all the time that he would go.

"Sure. Old Hal'll find one for you. Whynt you come on and go?"

Prew was looking around the bar. "I already said I'd go, dint I? Shut up on it. Drop it, for Christ's sake. Matter of fact, I meant to go all along. I was goin out to Waikiki to look you up, after I left here. What is this slop we drinkin anyway?"

A reader who was not already in the know would never figure out what Maggio and Prewitt are talking about here.

Sixty years later, *From Here to Eternity* has been published as Jones wrote it, and It is time now to bring all those G.I. hustlers who helped make the world safe for democracy out of the closet, and claim them as part of the gay community.

For starters I have assembled here a gallery of photographs depicting military men of the1940s, '50s and '60s in uniform, and out. It starts with some scene-setting images, showing men sleeping in a tent or lining up for short-arms inspection, or wandering about Times Square, and it ends with a celebration of the Peace; but most—not all, but most--of the pictures in between are nudes.

Photos showing naked men were illegal in this early era, but they were produced nonetheless by hobbyists who had cameras and darkrooms and models. The hobbyists sometimes distributed prints among friends, and friends of friends, and friends of friends of friends, and so the pictures got around.

The early enthusiasts produced snapshot-type work, but with experience a few became expert photographers, using props and poses and lighting and composition to produce very professional pictures. Some of them eventually became widely known under pseudonyms, such as Bruce of Los Angeles, Lon of New York, Douglas of Detroit, David of Cleveland and Kris of Chicago.

548

548: Well endowed, masculine male, mid-30's, executive, college grad, gay, quiet type. Interests: nude photography, develope and print my own pictures, sex, travel, good music, theater, stereo tape recording. Want to exchange letters and tapes with someone 18-35. Will show you a good time if you visit New Orleans, Baton Rouge, or Gulf Coast. Send photo. All letters answered. **LOUISIANA.**

After the War, as the gay community grew in numbers and strength, these brave photographers challenged the legal restrictions. Bob Mizer, who founded the Athletic Model Guild in 1945, tested the law by sending full-frontal nude pictures of men through the mail, and in 1947 he paid for his crime by serving a sentence of six months at Saugus Prison Farm.

Alonzo Hanagan (Lon of New York), was raided twice. The cops took all his cameras and darkroom equipment arid destroyed his prints and negatives. Lon took the hint, changed careers and became a piano teacher.

In the 1950s, Chuck Renslow (Kris Studios of Chicago) argued in court that men wearing skimpy posing straps were not nude so long as the cock and balls were covered. He won the case, and there instantly sprang up an entire industry of physique publications featuring models modestly attired in a string and a scrap of cloth.

Then the 1960s saw the arrival of nudist and naturalist publications, and by the end of the decade—the Stonewall era—male nude photography was protected by the First Amendment and physique photography flourished.

Now of course pornography is to be found everywhere, especially in the vast reaches of cyberspace, where a huge archive of vintage porn has escaped to the wild. That is where I have found many of the images included in the gallery.

Most of them are by anonymous artists, or at least by artists not known to me. However I include a few beautiful images (of fully clothed men) by Bob Mizer of the Athletic Model League. I also have one by Bruce Bellas (Bruce of Los Angeles), and several by Pat Milo, the most sensitive portraitist of them all. I may also have included other images by famous photographers without being aware of it.

Now, not all physique models were gay, let alone hustlers, so I cannot say for a fact that the men in these pictures were of the Private Maggio persuasion. I cannot even say for a fact that they were soldiers and sailors, even though they wear uniforms. After all, models can wear costumes. A cowboy hat does not turn a bodybuilder into a ranch hand, and a white cap does not make him a sailor.

But I invite you to take a look at them. Most of them do not look like regular beefcake models. They are not bodybuilders, and some of them even seem a little shy.

Generally they are wearing (or removing) entire uniforms, not just caps; and the clothes and shoes fit. It would take a military historian to identify all the uniforms and insignia and stripes worn by these men in these pictures, but the ones I do recognize are authentic.

Why the men wearing sailor uniforms outnumber three-to-one those of the other branches I cannot explain; I suppose it is because sailor uniforms are so darned cute.

G-39-25 SOUTHWEST — 26, 5'7", 170. Hobbies: art and photography. Would like to hear from truck drivers and anyone else for lasting friendships. Photo please.

Check out the sailors' high-waisted trousers with the thirteen buttons and the broadfall drop front. The sailors had to be handy with needle and thread to keep all those buttons attached.

Many of the men in these images have the single stripes of private, seaman and airman—the lowest ranks of enlisted men, and also the lowest paid, men like Prewitt and Maggio.

So although I cannot say for a fact that the men in these pictures are G.I. Hustlers, I can say that this is what G.I. Hustlers would look like when you got them home.

As Ulrichs said, they

Know not how goodly they are, the sight of them how overwhelming.

The hustler culture, I believe, has mostly disappeared from the U.S. military today, and it may be that the entire category of rough trade has pretty much faded away. In recent surveys, it seems, the pool of Kinsey 2's, 3's, 4's and 5's has dried up. Maybe so. It doesn't seem very likely to me, but who knows?

If so, health concerns probably have a lot to do with it. Another possibility is that it may be a result of a dawning awareness in the general population that getting a blowjob is just as homosexual as giving one. Or it could be that later investigators just are not as good as Kinsey at getting honest answers, and no real decline has occurred.

The Armed Services certainly have changed in other ways. Now they are an integrated force comprising all races, all sexes, and all sexualities. Another big change is that privates now get a base pay of $17,611 a year, with lots of extras depending upon recruiting incentives, so consequently they are less in need of outside sources of income.

However, the ancient customs still persist in some corners of the world. I recently received this communication from a friend in South America:

> **Here in Uruguay there is a lot of dealing with the police and military, because it is very easy to make an arrangement with them. Their pay is very low, and if you show them some money they will do anything. The gays from Argentina are surprised at this, because in Argentina it is not that way.**

> **The Fortaleza of Santa Teresa, where there is a military garrison and a campground, has turned into a Mecca of pilgrimage for gay tourism. All very covered-up, of course, and officially nothing is said.**

Soldier hustlers can still be found if you know where to look.

Of Greenbacks And Dress Blues

This was one of several pulp novels James. J. Proferes wrote for H. Lynn Womack's Guild Press. Some of his other titles were *Weep No More, My Laddie; Ungrateful Bastard; Hellbound in Leather; Any Man Is Fair Game; Seduction Seminar;* and *Don't Tempt Me.*

Womack had to close Guild Press in 1971 as part of an agreement with the F.B.I., in order to get his sentence for obscenity reduced from two-and-a-half years to six months.

Reproduced on the following pages are the cover and an advertisement for *Of Greenbacks and Dress Blues*, the tale of a sailor-hustler who insists he is not queer—and how he got his comeuppance.

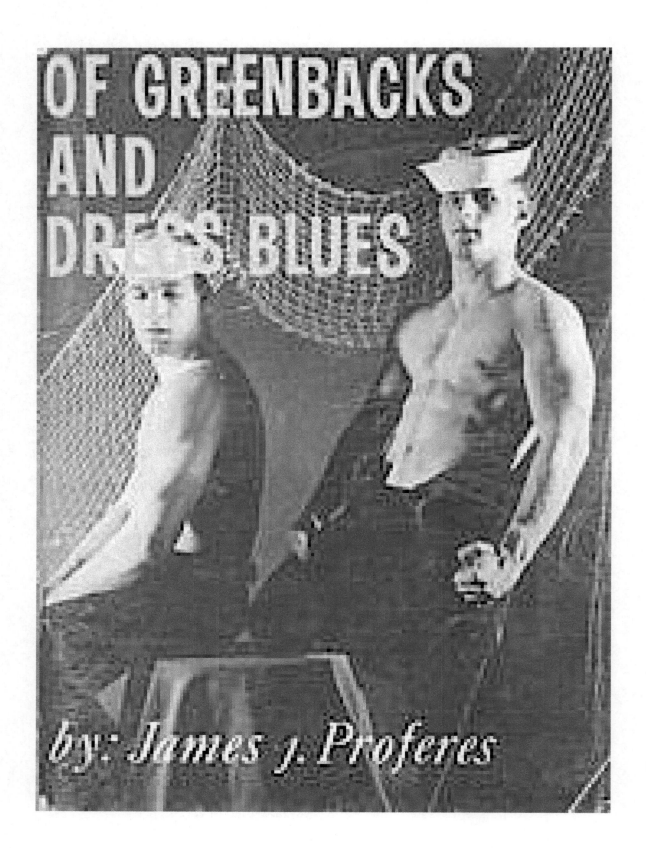

A BLAZING INTIMATE NOVEL
OF SAILORS · JOHNS · HUSTLERS !

An explosive novel that shows how hustling can lead a sailor to a degenerate life he enjoys!

OF GREENBACKS AND DRESS BLUES

3.00

Tim is a sailor stationed in Washington, D.C. While sitting in a bar, he recalls how he used to make extra spending money. "Each night he would go into the park, where the lonely men were, and for a few dollars would go home with them for a few hours to dispense their favors."

At the Lamplighter Club he meets a handsome older man. Says Tim: "I don't want to lead you on; I have to go with someone who is willing to pay."

Soon Tim learns that hustling can have its pitfalls. He's picked up by a wealthy man who wants Tim to go all the way. "I'll show you who is queer!" The youth was crying as he brought his fists down on the man who now lay under him.

Tim realizes what he really is when he meets a 15-year-old kid. What follows leaves no doubts in Tim's mind as to what his real sex interest is.

Tim would lie back and enjoy the johns who took his body hungrily, but little did he know how exciting a young boy could be until it was too late for him to return to the straight world!

ORDER BLANK

Send Coupon to: **GUILD BOOK SERVICE**, P.O. Box 7410, Franklin Station, Washington, D.C. 20044.

Enclosed is $_____ to cover the cost of_____ copies of **OF GREENBACKS AND DRESS BLUES** at the sensational price of $3.00 per copy.

Name _____

Address _____

City _____ State _____ Zip Code _____

Please use your Zip Code

By

J. J.

Proferes

Ad in the Grecian Guild Quarterly, May 1967

19

The Gallery

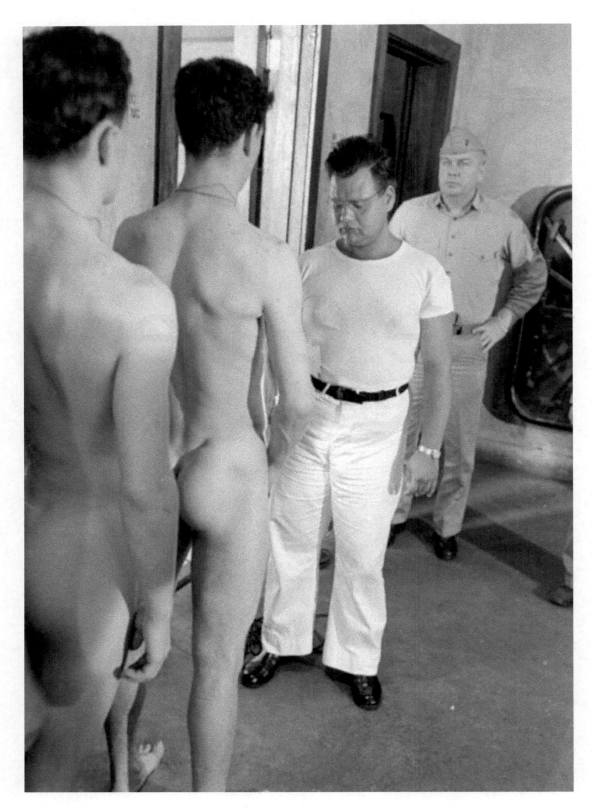

Short-Arms Inspection

Sleeping in a Tent

**"Couple of Sailors Wait Around Paramount Theater
for Something to Show Up."**

"Soldiers Cluster in 'Island' in Square, Underneath Roosevelt Profile."

Times Square

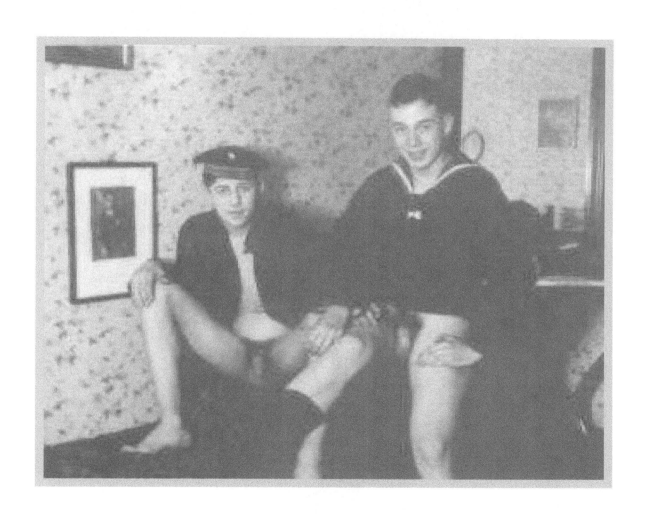

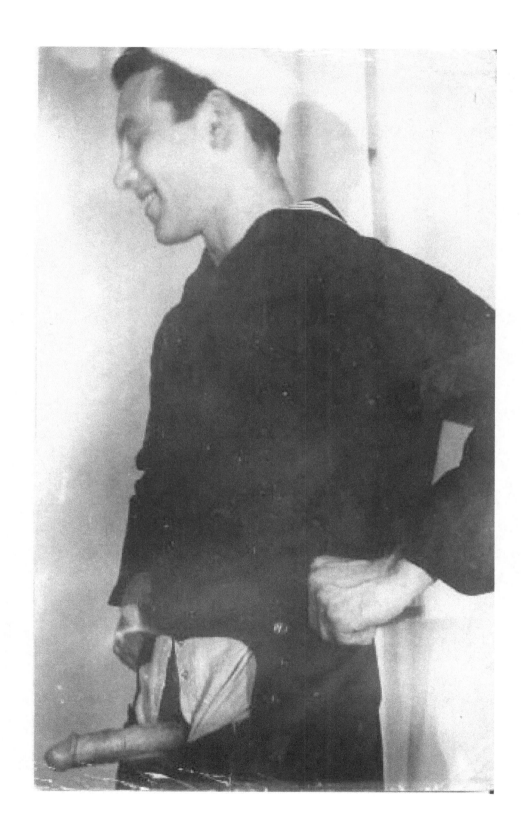

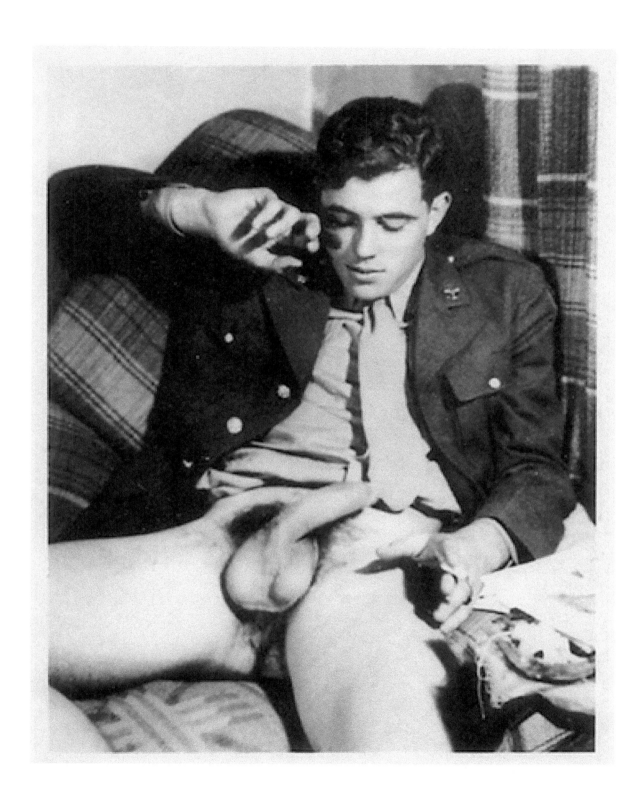

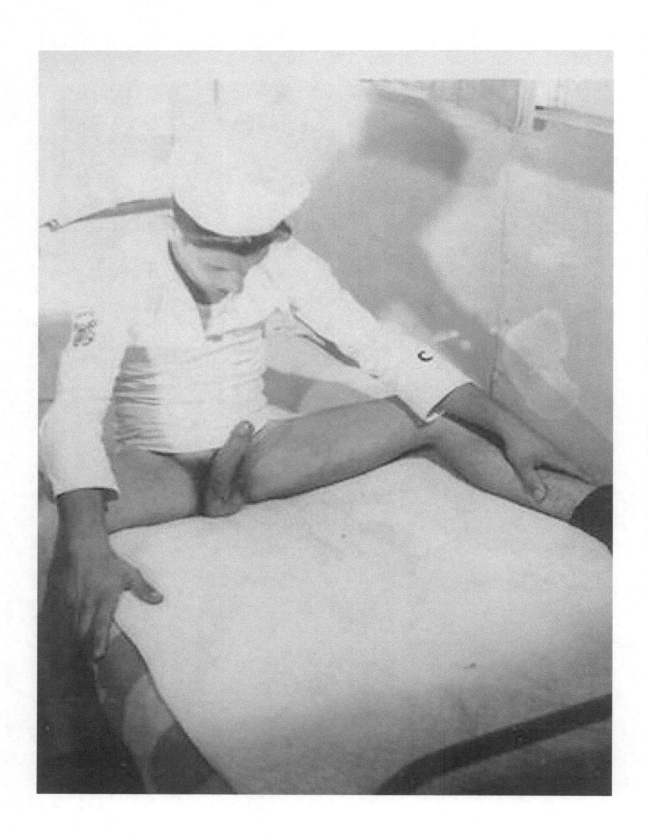

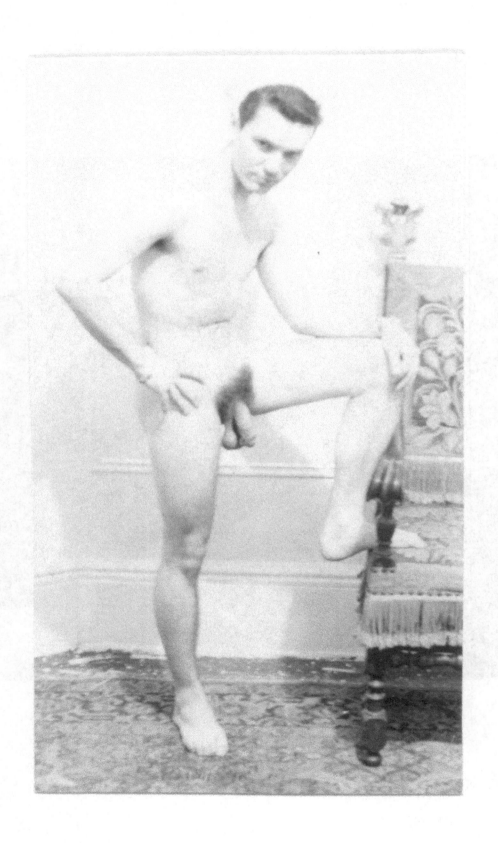

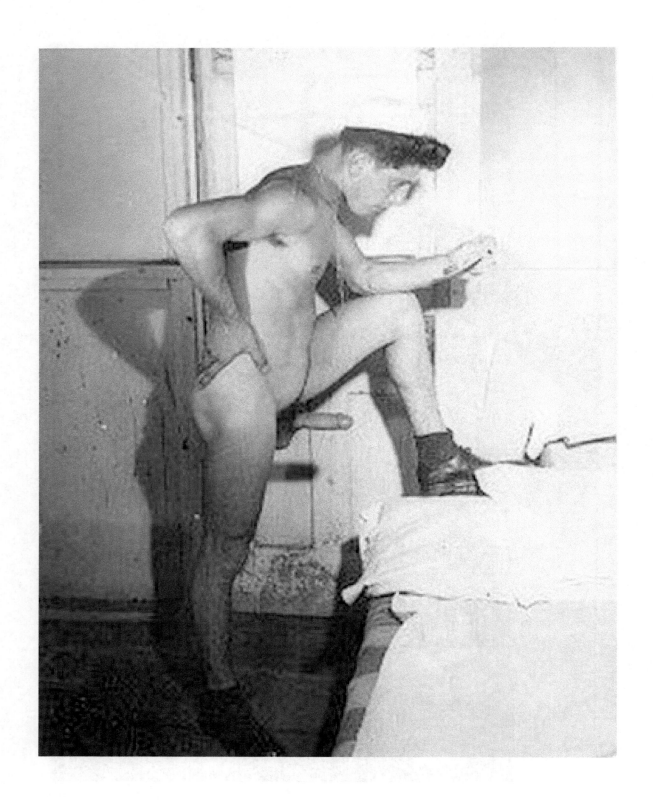

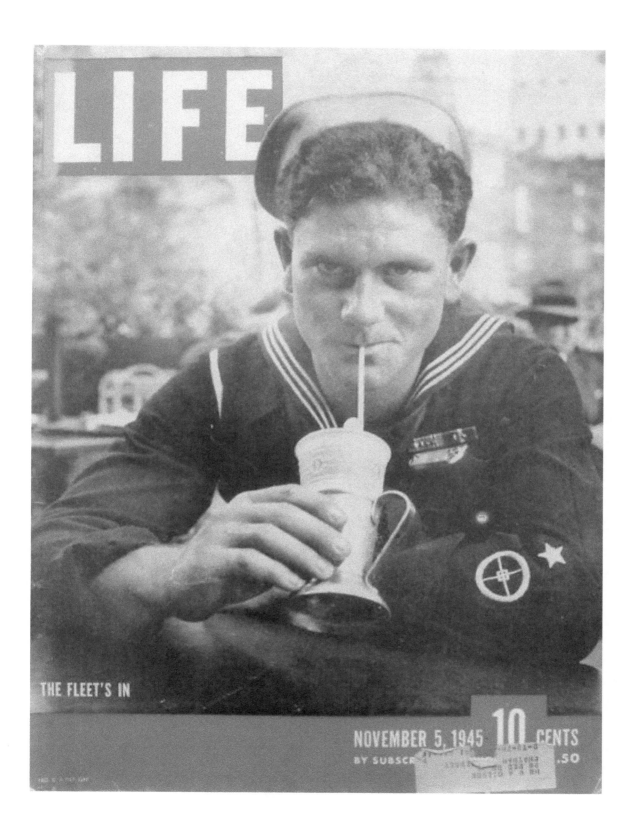

LIFE

THE FLEET'S IN

NOVEMBER 5, 1945 10 CENTS

BY SUBSCR... .50

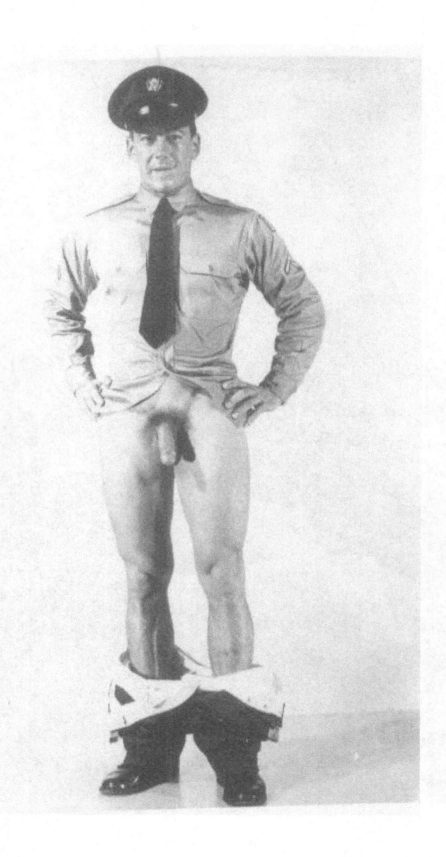

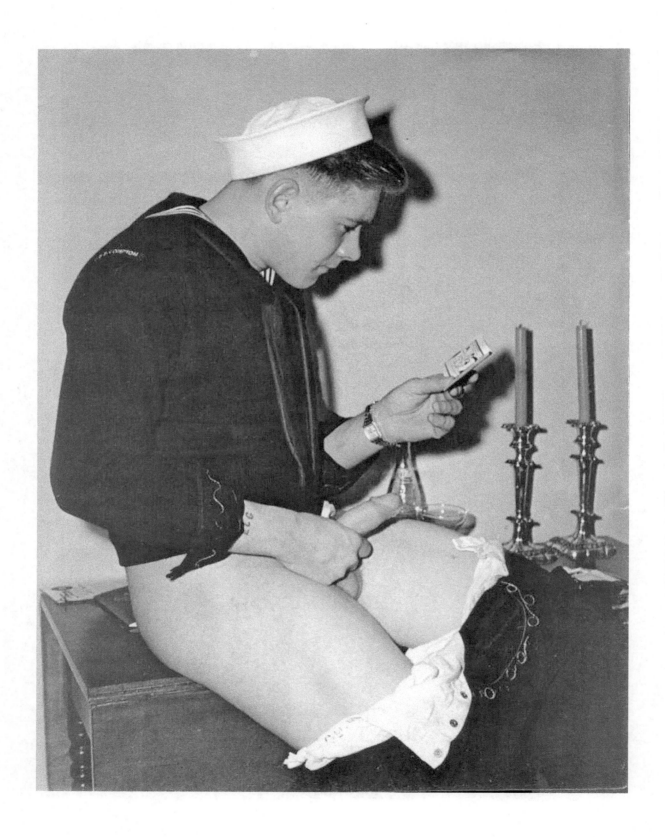

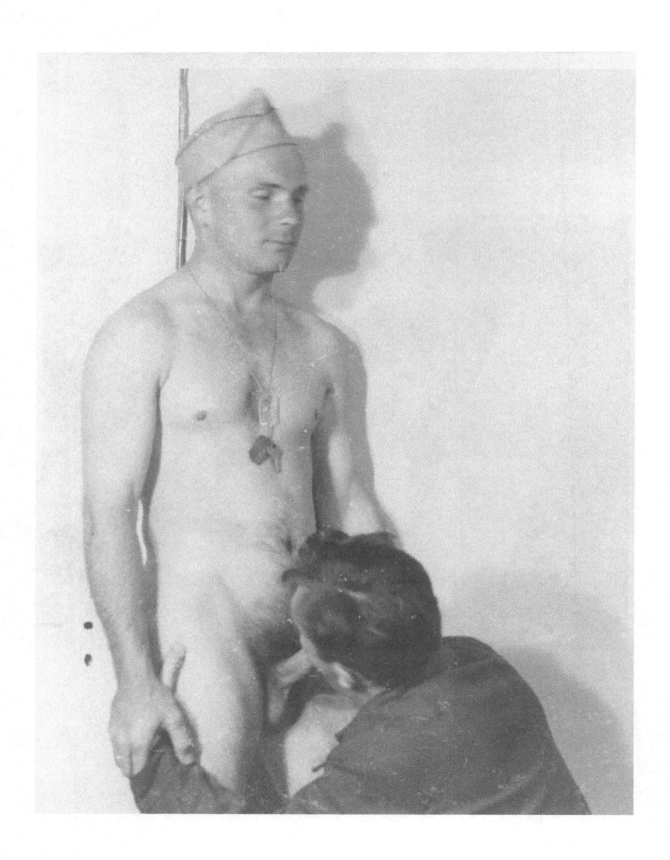

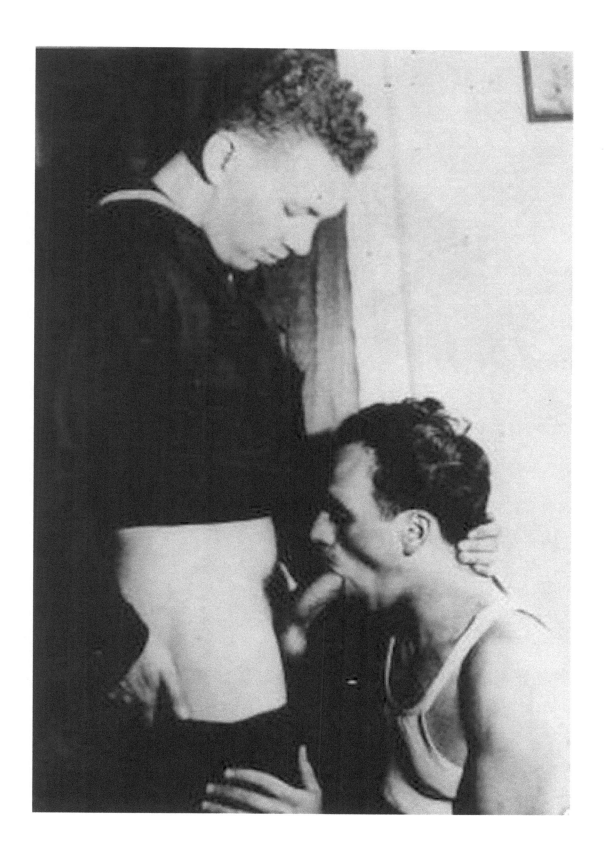

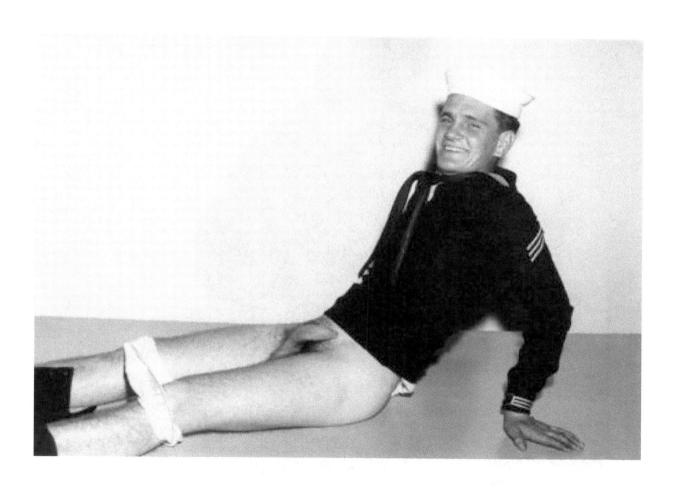

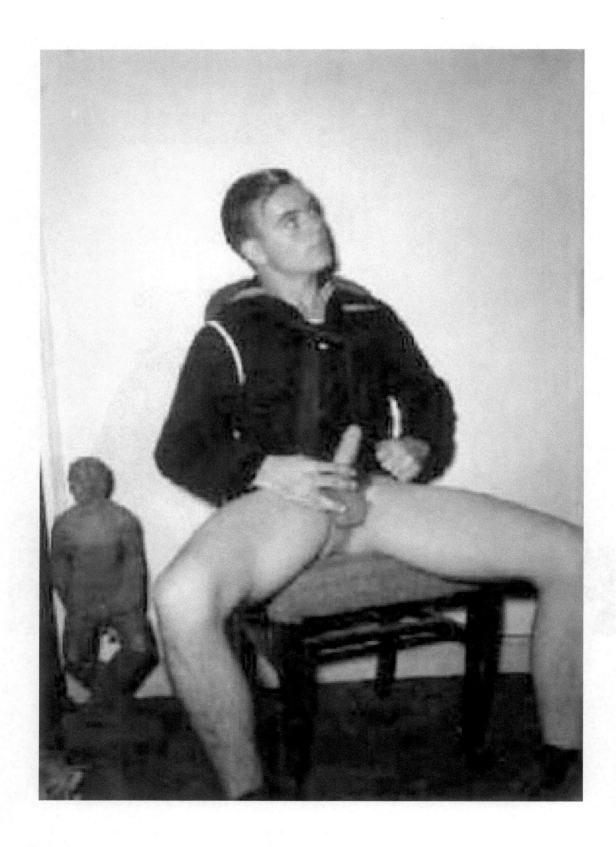

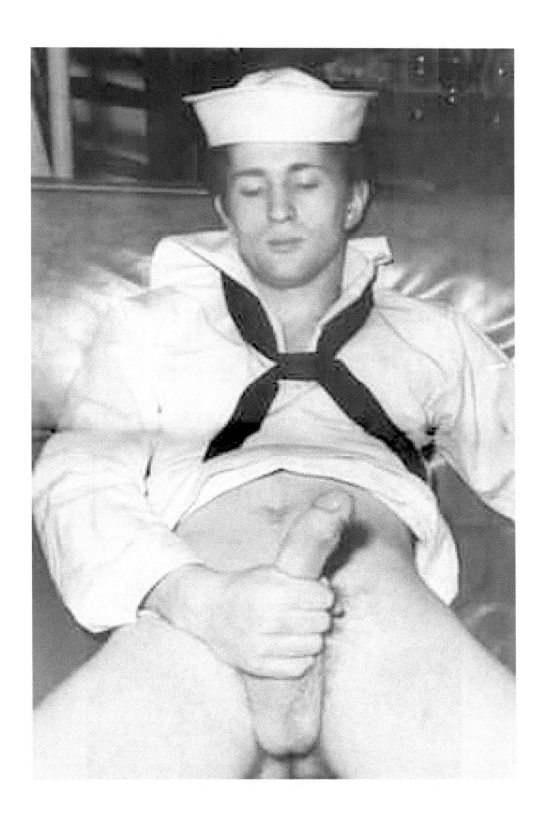

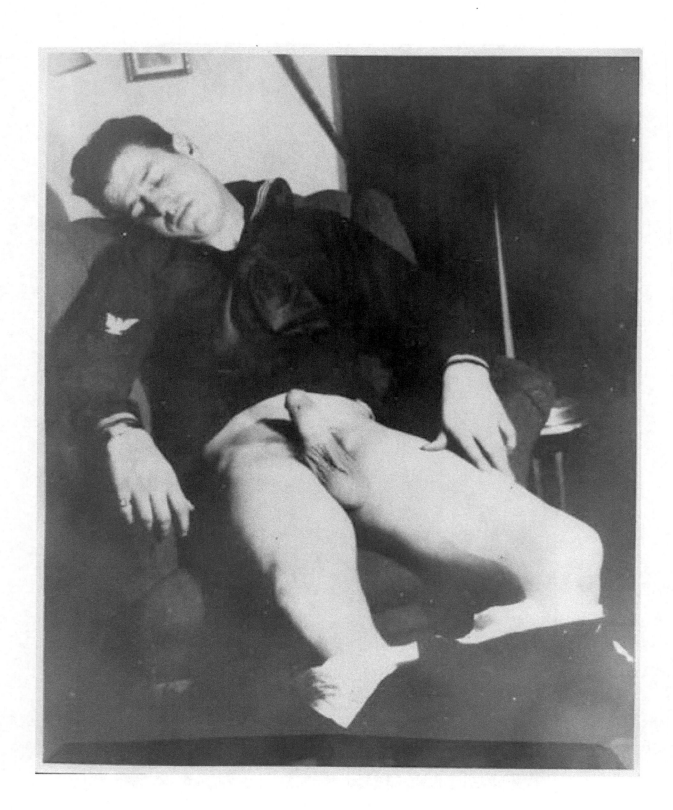

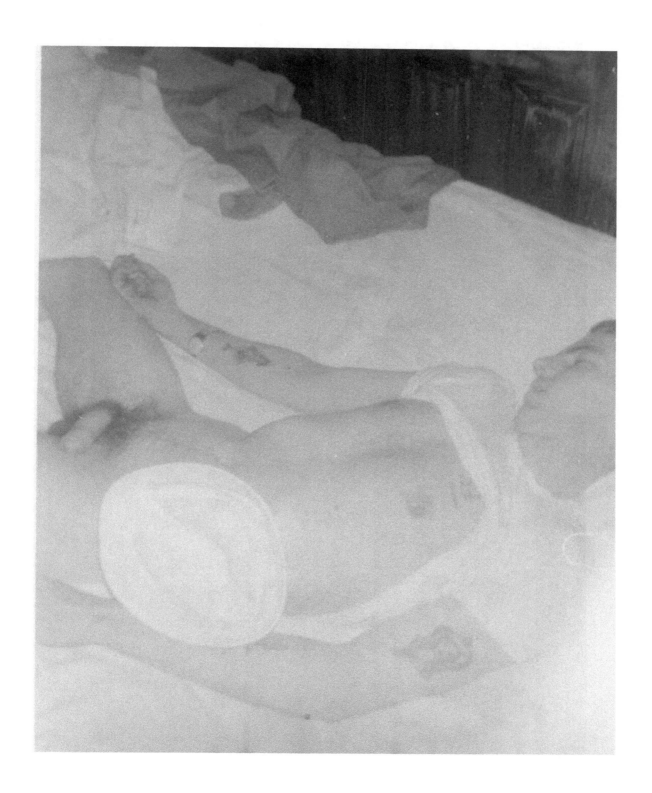

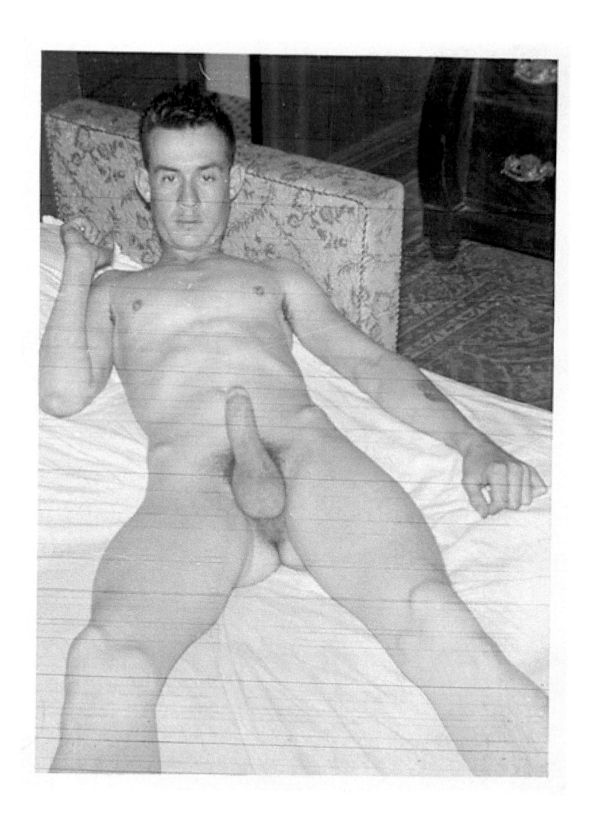

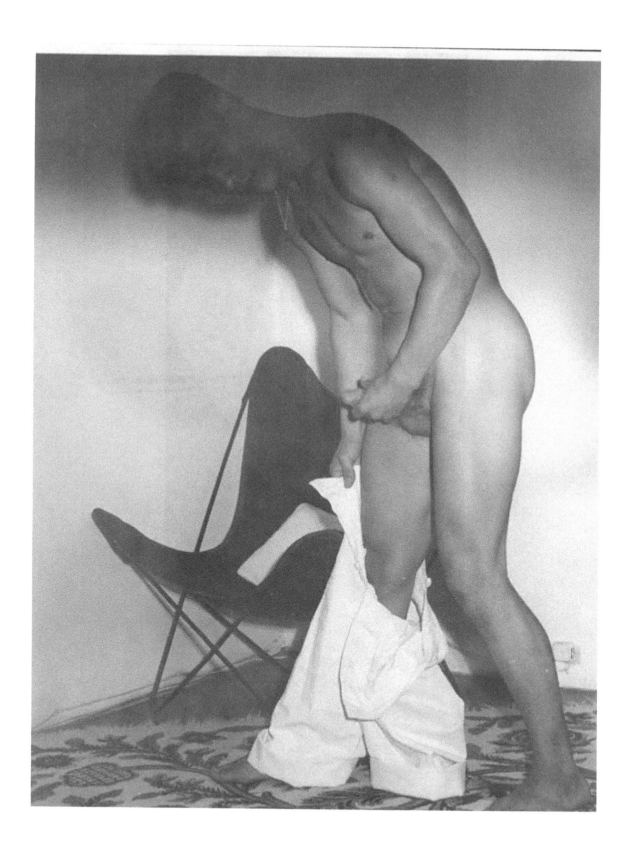

one

AUGUST 1963

FIFTY CENTS

THE HOMOSEXUAL VIEWPOINT

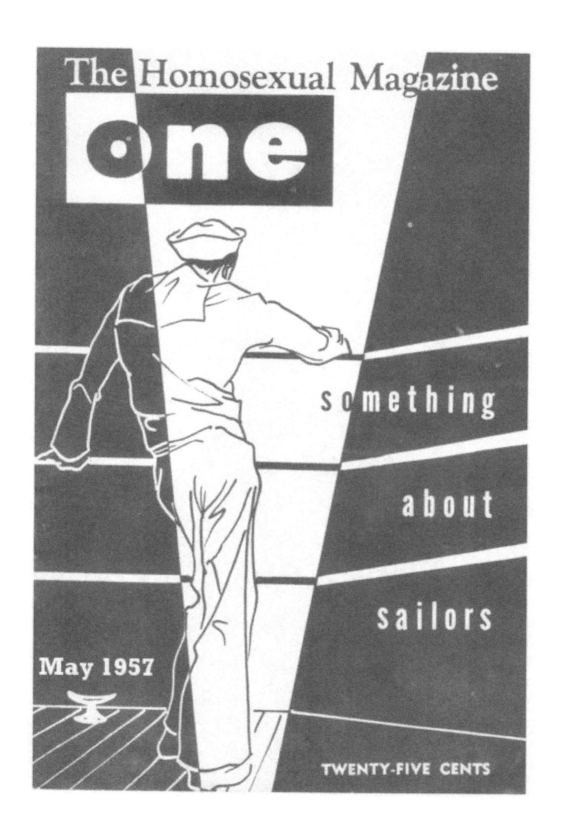

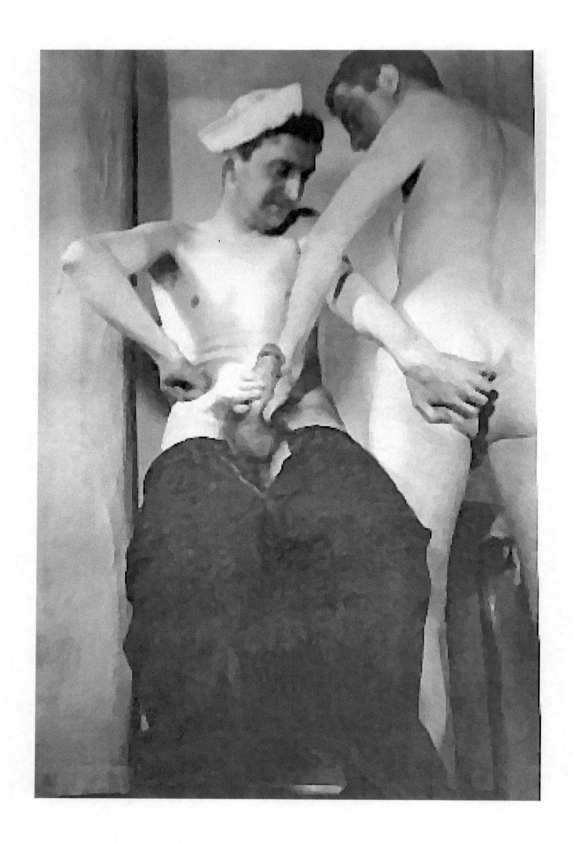

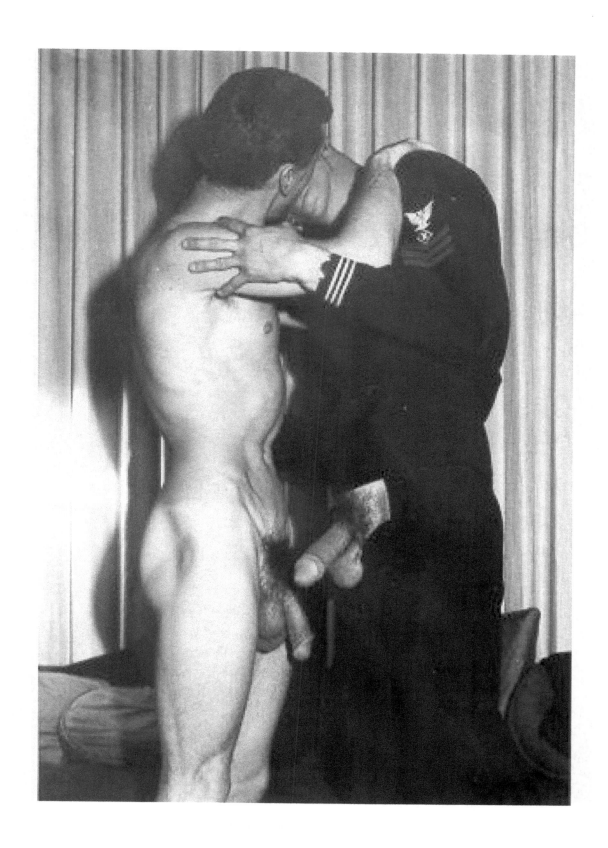

Athletic Model Guild

Athletic Model Guild

Athletic Model Guild

Athletic Model Guild

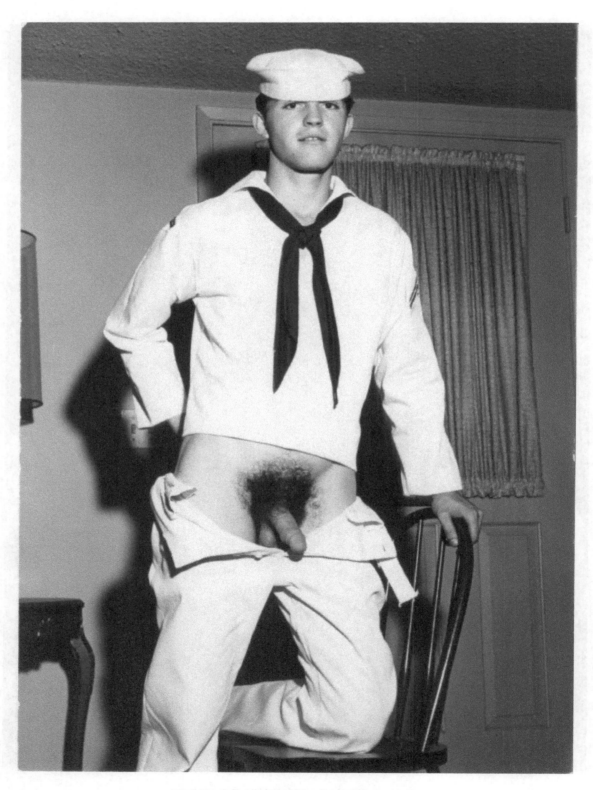

Mel Bates by Bruce of Los Angeles

by Pat Milo

Marvin Bennett by Pat Milo

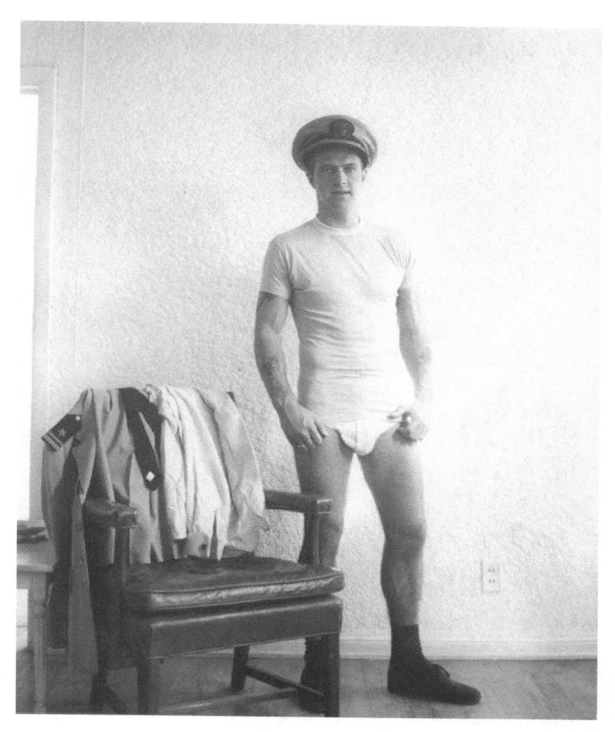

Charlie Day by Pat Milo

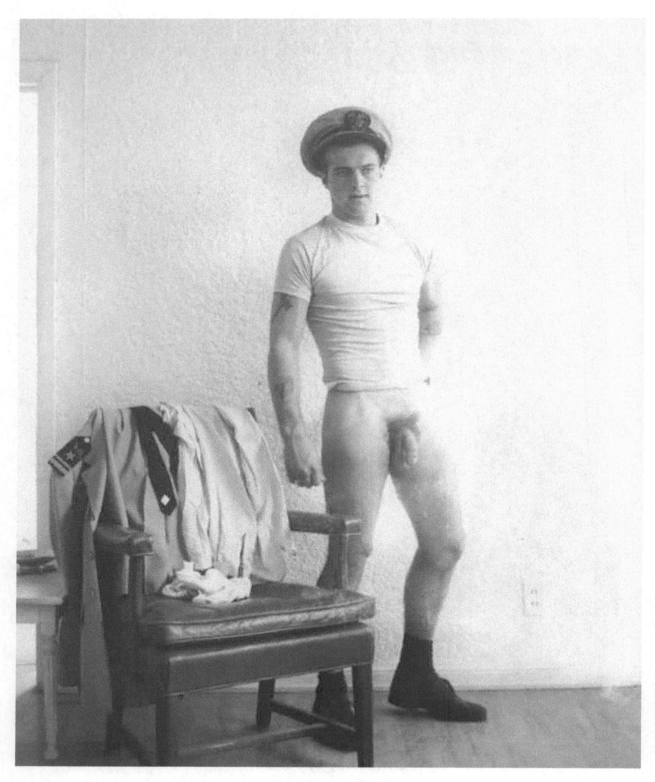

Charlie Day, by Pat Milo

Charlie Day, by Pat Milo

83

Dave Allen by Kris Studio

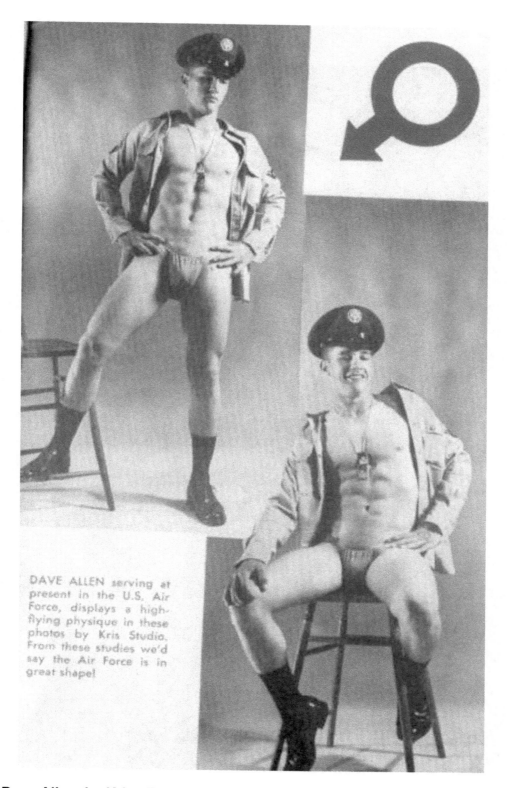

DAVE ALLEN serving at
present in the U.S. Air
Force, displays a high-
flying physique in these
photos by Kris Studio.
From these studies we'd
say the Air Force is in
great shape!

**Dave Allen, by Kris. The posing briefs were not regular Air Force issue,
but were required to get the magazine through the mails in the 1950s.**

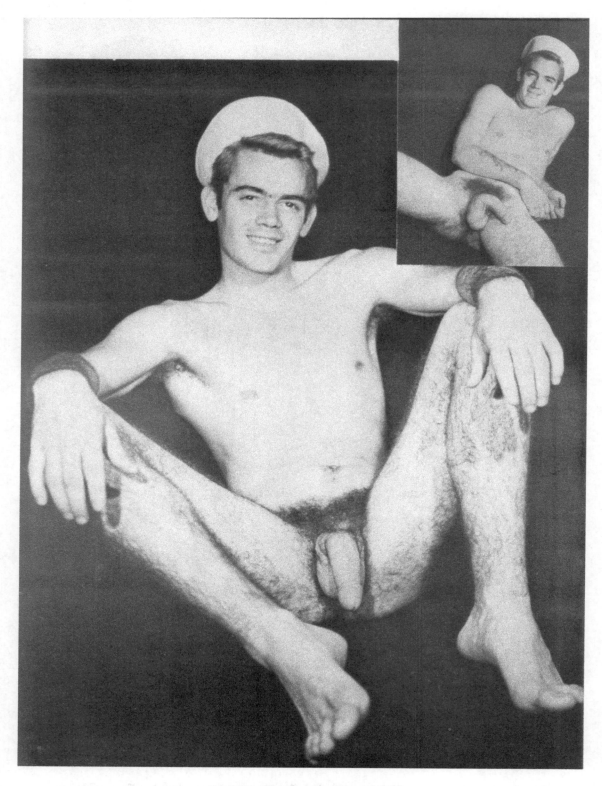

Carl Smith, Saxon #2, 1969

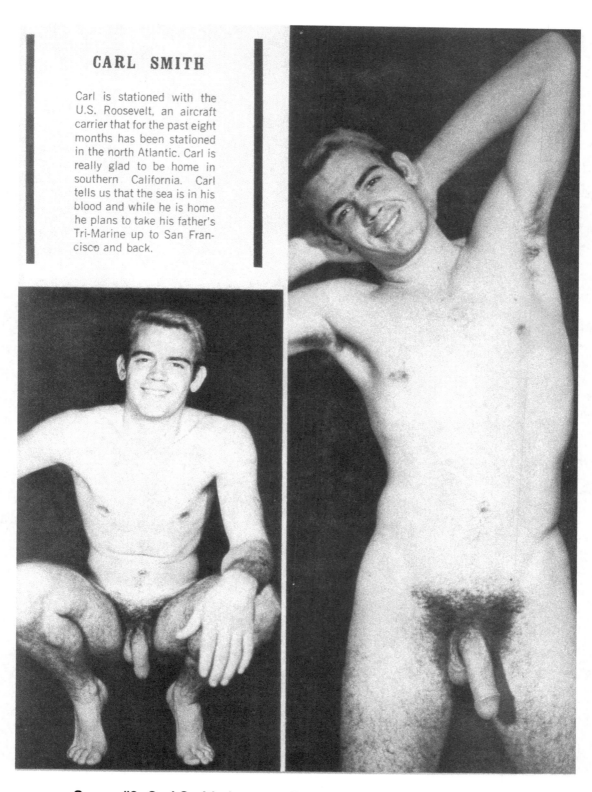

CARL SMITH

Carl is stationed with the U.S. Roosevelt, an aircraft carrier that for the past eight months has been stationed in the north Atlantic. Carl is really glad to be home in southern California. Carl tells us that the sea is in his blood and while he is home he plans to take his father's Tri-Marine up to San Francisco and back.

Saxon #2: Carl Smith, home on leave from the U.S.S. Roosevelt.

Times Square

References

Chauncey, George, *Gay New York*. (New York: Basic Books, 1994)

Hyde, H. Montgomery, *The Love That Dared Not Speak Its Name*. (Boston: Little, Brown, 1970)

Jennie June. *Autobiography of an Androgyne*. (New York: Medico-Legal Journal, 1919)

Jennie June. *The Female-Impersonators*. (New York: Medico-Legal Journal, 1922)

Kaiser, Charles, *The Gay Metropolis*. (New York: Houghton Mifflin, 1997)

Kennedy, Hubert, *Ulrichs*. (Boston: Alyson Publications, 1988)

Kinsey, Alfred C., Pomeroy Wardell B., and Martin, Clyde E., *Sexual Behavior in the Human Male*. (Philadelphia and London: W. B. Saunders Company, 1948).

Loughery, John, *The Other Side of Silence*. (New York: Henry Holt and Company, 1998)

Nerf, Swasarnt. *Gay Guides for 1949*, edited by Hugh Hagius. (New York: Bibliogay, 2010.)

Reay, Barry, *New York Hustlers: Masculinity and Sex in Modern America*. (Manchester University Press, 2010)

Many of the images in this book were downloaded from the internet. Regular web protocol is to acknowledge the source with a link, which I was not able to do because I wrote for print. But I do want to mention several blogs where I found inspiration and some beautiful images: on Blogspot, Dream-Exchange; and on Tumblr, Purelyvintagegay, Vinboz, Morphodite, RandyDandy and Zenfancy.

Milton Keynes UK
Ingram Content Group UK Ltd.
UKHW012238080924
1544UKWH00020B/35

9 780615 475813